BIBLE STORIES
ACCORDING TO
TUFFY TURTLE

BIBLE STORIES
ACCORDING TO

In the beginning God created

TUFFY TURTLE

WRITTEN BY JONI LUNDIN MCNAMARA
ILLUSTRATIONS BY SUSAN STANLEY

XULON PRESS

Xulon Press
2301 Lucien Way #415
Maitland, FL 32751
407.339.4217
www.xulonpress.com

Unless otherwise indicated, Scripture quotations taken from the New Revised Standard Version (NRSV). Copyright © 1989 the Division of Christian Education of the National Council of the Churches of Christ in the United States of America.

Printed in the United States of America.
Edited by Xulon Press

ISBN: 9781545616659

Table of Contents

Bible Stories according to Tuffy Turtle

Introduction

Once upon a time in the land of Faith-Coming, there lived a very old and very wise turtle named Tuffy. Tuffy had lived for many, many years, and he was the beginning of a long line of distinguished Faith Turtles who would be known to pass down the wisdom of the ages . . . the truth about the Creator of All that was, is, and ever will be.

These are the stories of this special family of Turtles, known as Spiriturtlelus, ("Spir-it-tur-tle-lus") from the Beginning of Time to the coming of the Special One, the Son of the Creator God.

You see, Tuffy was the first of a long—a very long—line of Faith Teachers. He was the great, great, great, great-grandfather of the Tuffy of Abraham, and the great, great, great, great, great, great, great, great-grandfather of the Tuffy who lived during the time of Moses, and the great, great, great . . . well, you get the picture, right?

This very first Tuffy lived in a tiny glen in the Garden of Abundance and Beauty, and then on the outskirts of a great forest. But even so, he was well-known by the all the animals, who often came to him for advice and knowledge—and most of all—to learn of the Creator and how to obtain the magic called "Faith."

Bible Stories according to Tuffy Turtle

Now Tuffy never, ever called Faith "magic," but to some of his forest friends, they just couldn't get it. Take one, for example, by the name of J.R.—J.R. Rabbit.

J.R., for all his pranks and tricks that he tried to pull on the other animals, was a very nice rabbit for the most part. But his playful nature didn't do him any good, and because of this playful nature, he just couldn't seem to come to terms with faith.

"But ya gotta see it to believe it!" he would often say to Tuffy.

You see, J.R. was the first of a very long line of skeptics. In fact, his family name became known as Skeptirabbitus ("Skep-ti-rab-bit-us") and it went all the way through Biblical times too. Yes, that's a very long, long time.

He was the great, great, great, great, great, great, great, great-grandfather—well, you get the picture—of the J.R. Rabbit who was around during the time of Moses. And another great, great, great, great, great . . . yes, you got it . . . who was around during the time of the Hebrew Judges, Deborah, Samson, and Gideon to name a few.

There were many of these Skeptirabbituses around throughout history, and they all were rather playful (always playing pranks). They were also always doubtful of anything they couldn't see or understand.

So you see, Tuffy and J.R.'s descendants travelled through history together. The Spiriturtleluses told the story of the Great Creator and His Love for His Creation, and the Skeptirabbituses questioned everything.

But let's start from the beginning with our stories of Tuffy and his family of Spiriturtleluses, and we won't forget the J.R.s of history too!

Dedication

I can think of no one better to dedicate this book to
than to the Triune God,
Our Father who creates us,
Jesus who sets the example to follow and saves us,
and the
Holy Spirit who leads, guides, fills us, and inspires us.

Of course, I also cannot help but to
dedicate this work of love to the
Love of my life, my husband, Robert Patrick,
and to our two most extraordinary children,
Deborah Carlyn and Robert Lundin,
who showered me with their love
and patience!
And who always supported me in
following my dreams....

Acknowledgements

It is hard to know where to begin as there have been so many people who have inspired and encouraged me over the years, and, frankly, just plain put up with me with the myriad of characters and stories running around in my head. From all the puppeteers with GEM PUPPET PRODUCTIONS/ ARK ANGEL PUPPETS, (far too many to name!), to my various partners, especially Gigi Galloway who challenged me and helped me grow creatively, and to all who spent hours developing characters and plays with me.

I am especially thankful for my husband, Bob, who never quite knew who he was coming home to when we were in production and rehearsing for a show! And, of course, my two children, Deb and Rob, who were patient, especially in those trying teen years when their mother was off creating another character or show - and making them be part of it! Many thanks to my mom's caregivers, Nancy Dyer and Dean Wood, who read the scripts And stores and encouraged me to continue; and to Mary Peraro, my first editor who shared her years of educational training and expertise with me. I cannot be thankful enough to Susan Stanley, my most gifted and talented illustrator and friend, who brought these characters to life on paper. It's one thing to make a character come alive as a puppet, but something else to capture their personality and essence on paper!

I am grateful to all for their help and love over the 40-plus years of playing with "multiple personalities" in creating these plays and stories. I cannot forget to mention Cindy Engalla of Xulon Press who called me during a very trying time when my mother was in the process of dying and asked if she and the staff could pray for us. It was very meaningful to me and was the incentive to continue to pursue publishing my stories with Xulon.

And of course, the biggest source of inspiration came from our Creator alone. I cannot have written anything without the inspiration and guidance of the Holy Spirit who filled me and inspired me to share the Good News of God's Love and involvement in His Creation whenever and wherever I could. Thanks be to God!

Book 1: Creation

Chapter 1

The Great Beginning

When the earth was young and green, there was the Garden of Abundance and Beauty, a true Garden of Plenty. There were plants of all kinds, trees of every shape, flowers of every color, and silence. The Great Creator of All (who didn't have a name yet) was pleased with His work, but the silence was . . . well, it just wasn't right to the Creator's ears.

So He created animals of all sizes, shapes, and sounds, and among His most favorite was a little turtle the Creator called "Tuffy."

Now, Tuffy was tiny and green, and he seemed to blend in to the grass and shrubs. He was often stepped on by the other bigger animals. So the Great Creator gave Tuffy a hard shell that would protect him from the larger animals.

Tuffy wanted to thank the Great Creator, but being young, he couldn't speak very clearly and so instead of saying "Great Creator," he came up with an easy name, "God," so the Great Creator became known to all the animals in the Garden of Plenty as God.

Now, you might ask, how did this happen? Well, Tuffy was so thankful and happy that he was protected by his new shell that God had given him, he just had to tell all the animals. Every one of them was amazed at what they heard.

Every one of the animals learned to be grateful and to thank God for what they had. They loved how different they were from the others. They loved that God had made them not just differently, but special.

The lion loved his big, flowing mane, and the lioness was proud of her hunting skills. And they thanked God.

The giraffes loved their long, slender necks, their long eyelashes, and their long tongues that could reach the highest leaves on the trees. They thanked God.

The cheetahs loved their spots and their speed! Oh, how they loved their speed. They thanked God.

The elephants loved their size, their gentle nature, and their memories. Oh yes, they never forgot to thank God for being elephants!

The Great Beginning

The birds of all sizes and colors thanked God for the ability to fly and for the songs they sang. They raised their songs in thanksgiving to God.

All the animals were thankful for the music they brought to the Garden of Plenty.

Of course, there were some birds like ostriches and turkeys that didn't sing or fly like the others, but they were large and fast, and they were thankful for that!

The larger animals, like the donkey . . . well, they just thanked God for being alive!

The larger animals like the bears were thankful that they were . . . well, large! Some were thankful that they could sleep all winter long.

The smaller, furrier animals like the skunks, possums, mice, and lambs all were thankful to the Creator God too. They were given the special gifts of warm, fluffy fur, bushy tails, soft, wooly coats, and of being tiny and swift. They all came to know, love, and praise God for all that He had given them.

All except one, that is. One little rabbit had . . . well, shall we say . . . he had a rather skeptical, playful—even prankful—attitude. He became known as J.R. Tuffy called him Jack Rabbit, but the animals of the Garden of Plenty called him Jack Rascal!

Now, J.R. really meant no harm to anyone, but often his little pranks got him into trouble with some of the animals.

Often Tuffy would come to his rescue and explain to him about life in the Garden. He tried to get J.R. to understand how the Great Creator God made everything and everyone to live in harmony and peace together.

The Great Beginning

"Harmony!" J.R. would say. "Let the birds sing in harmony! I want to play and have fun, like when I pretended to find magic pine cones. Remember that?" he asked Tuffy.

Tuffy would reply, "Yes, I remember that you learned a lesson from the others when you tried to take and hide all their food. When they found out, you lost not only all that you had hidden, but you lost their respect and their friendship."

"Oh yeah, and you came to my rescue by saying that that 'God' of yours wouldn't like them to be mean to me," J.R. would remind him.

"Well, it wasn't exactly like that," Tuffy would say. "I explained that God created us all to live together and get along together and that you were just as special as the others. God still loved you even though you liked to"—Tuffy cleared his throat—"even though you liked to play pranks."

"Well, what's life if there's not some fun in it!" J.R. would reply. "I make the animals laugh."

"You make the animals angry," Tuffy would say.

"Ah, that's nothing. They always come around after you talk to them."

"But someday I may not be here to help you," Tuffy would say.

"What! Are you going away?" would ask a startled J.R.

"No, I have everything right here in our Garden. But someday God might ask you what have you done with your life to help others."

Now here is where we have our problem with J.R. He was the first of what came to be known as the Skeptirabbitus family. He just couldn't understand what Tuffy was talking about. He couldn't "see" God.

"Tuffy, there you go again about this 'God' thing," he would say. "I don't get it. Where is this God? Why don't we see Him? Why don't I see Him if He's so important to me?"

Tuffy would try to explain that he had to have faith in the One who created everything, Faith in the One who made all the animals special in His sight, Faith in the one and only God of Creation. But J.R. just couldn't get it.

"I can see the trees," J.R. would say. "I can smell the flowers. I can eat the lettuce and carrots in the garden. I can hop faster than the wolf that chases me. But where is this God that I'm supposed to thank for all this, and that I'm supposed to have faith in?"

"Do you feel the breeze ruffle your fur?" Tuffy would ask.

"Yes . . . so?" J.R. would respond.

The Great Beginning

"Well, that is like God. You feel the presence of the breeze but you cannot see it. When you have faith, you feel the presence of God even though you cannot see Him. So be thankful for the breeze that you cannot see, and be thankful for the God that you cannot see."

Tuffy tried to show and explain to J.R. the mystery of God. But being the first of the family of Skeptirabbitus, J.R. just couldn't get it.

And what about this family of Skeptirabbituses? Well, that's another story for another day.

Chapter 2

Get Out, Get Going, Get a Life (The Expulsion)

Something was wrong—dreadfully wrong. Tuffy could feel it. He didn't know what exactly, but something had happened in the Garden of Abundance. All the animals were quiet. The birds had stopped singing. No animals were moving about. It was a strange, strange quiet.

Quiet? Well, not exactly. All had heard the voice of the Creator God, and He was not happy. He was scolding those new creatures called man and woman who had been given the names Adam and Eve. They had done something that had angered the Creator, but Tuffy didn't know what.

Like all the animals of the Garden of Abundance, he had stayed quiet in his shell, waiting . . . waiting for the Creator to tell him what had happened. He didn't know how or why, but he knew that the Creator would let him know in the Creator's own way and in the Creator's own time.

Then the tapping began. Well, it was more like a soft pounding on his shell. And he heard the whisper.

"Tuffy, are you in there?" he heard J.R. Rabbit whisper.

Tuffy could see J.R. leaning his head into his shell. J.R. was shaking, his ears drooping, his eyes wide.

"Yes, I'm here, J.R.," Tuffy said. "What is it? What do you want?" he asked.

"Want!" whined J.R., his voice trembling. "I want to know if you know what I know!"

Slowly Tuffy came out of his shell and took a long look at J.R., who was not the cocky, self-assured, fun-loving rabbit he normally was.

He was shaking and quaking, and was just not his normal self—whatever that really was, as Tuffy was still trying to figure out this strange rabbit.

Get Out, Get Going, Get A Life (the Expulsion)

"Did you hear it? Did you hear that strange voice talking to those strange creatures?" asked J.R., trying to compose himself. "They did something they weren't supposed to," he continued, sounding bit more like his cocky self then.

"What do you mean?" asked Tuffy, curious that somehow J.R. seemed to know what had happened.

"Well, you know how you told me these humans could eat anything in our garden, just like the rest of us, but that they couldn't eat from some special tree?"

Tuffy nodded. "Yes, they weren't to eat from the "Tree of Knowledge of Good and Evil."

"Well, they did," J.R. whispered as he looked slowly over his shoulder.

"That voice! I **never** heard a voice like that. I thought I was gonna fall over dead from the sound! The earth shook! Why I could barely stand up!" J.R. looked around again and over Tuffy's shell, as if afraid of something or someone, Tuffy thought.

"Yes, J.R., I heard the voice; it was the voice of the Creator that I've been telling you about."

"Creator! This, this God you want me to believe in?" J.R. looked at Tuffy curiously.

"You always talk of this Creator being a good, kind, and loving God. But He sure wasn't this afternoon. He was angry, in a strange sort of way."

"What do you mean?" asked Tuffy, curious to know what J.R. had seen and heard. "Exactly what happened? How do you know they ate from the Tree?"

"Well, I saw it all! I was there. The woman, Eve, said she was tempted to pull one of those big red fruits from the tree, and so she did, and she shared it with that guy, Adam."

They seemed to enjoy it, but then the voice . . . that Voice came, and they got afraid and tried to hide." J.R. took a deep breath and continued, more calmly now. "It didn't do them any good to hide though, 'cause that Voice seemed to know where they were and asked why they had covered themselves up with leaves."

"Leaves?" asked Tuffy, curious.

"Yeah, I guess they were trying to hide in the bushes, but it didn't work. Then the Voice asked why they had eaten from the one Tree they had been told not to eat from. I don't know what the big deal was, but that Voice wasn't happy about it."

"No, I suppose not," said Tuffy, slowly shaking his head in sadness.

He knew that the Creator had given everything that the creatures, animals, and humans needed. If the Creator told them not to eat something—and all the animals knew what they were to eat and what they were not to eat—well, they knew and obeyed.

Tuffy was silent as he thought, *But these humans, Adam and Eve, they were different indeed.*

"Well, they ate this fruit," J.R. continued, "and then they blamed each other for doing it. Well, Eve blamed some snake, and Adam blamed Eve, and the next thing I heard, they were told to leave the Garden." J.R. shook his head.

"Imagine that. Where are they gonna go? I didn't know there was anything other than this Garden. I mean, who would want to leave it?"

J.R. cocked his head, shaking it, and sounded a bit more like his old self.

By this time, Tuffy was already walking toward that fateful tree. He had to see and hear for himself what had happened. It wasn't that he didn't believe J.R., for he did, but somehow he knew that life was going to be very different from now on. He didn't know how he knew, but he just knew.

He got to the grove where The Tree of Knowledge of Good and Evil was, and there he saw Adam and Eve huddled together, saddened and   crying.

He heard the Creator's Voice telling them that they must now work the ground, plant their own food, care for their own crops, and hunt for their food.

Work . . . work? That was a new concept for no one had to work for their food in the Garden of Abundance and Beauty. God cared for and provided everything.

Somehow, Tuffy's fate and future would be tied to the fate of Adam and Eve. He knew that he would be leaving the Garden of Abundance and Beauty with them. He didn't know how he knew, he just knew.

He looked to his side, and there was J.R. standing next to him. If Tuffy could have smiled, he would have, for he knew that J.R. would be part of this new life outside the Garden. He didn't know how he knew, he just knew.

Chapter 1

Time to Learn

This is the story of the seventh generation of Tuffy Turtle's family, and how Tuffy came to be with Noah and his family. It's hard to say whether Noah chose Tuffy or Tuffy chose Noah, or if some higher Power chose them both.

But of course, we know that it was this higher Power from the beginning of time that had chosen the first turtle and his descendants to tell the animals of the world about the Creator God, "God" being the name that the first Tuffy Turtle had called the Creator of All that Is.

As our story opens, it was a bright and sunny day, as it usually was in the land of two rivers. But something was different about this day. The birds who had been singing happily all morning were now quiet as they watched the activity taking place with interest. A tiny little turtle also watched from where he was hiding in the reeds along the riverbank.

They watched with interest as Noah and his three sons gathered wood, cut it, and put it all together. This had been going on for several days, and today it looked like they were building a boat. A big boat. A **huge** boat. And it was very different from the little two-man boats that were used for fishing along the river. This was a HUGE, HUGE boat!

The little turtle wondered what and why they would do such a thing. That boat was too big to even fit in the river!

He thought he'd go to his grandfather, a very old and wise turtle who, so it was said, had been given special powers and knowledge by the Great Creator God. Surely he would know.

Tuffy found his grandfather sunning himself on a rock by the riverbank.

"Grandfather, why is Noah building that big boat?" he asked. "It's too, too big for our river."

"Ah, my little one, I am glad you came to ask. It is time for you to know that you will be going on a trip with Noah on that big boat."

"But Grandfather, he doesn't need to build a big boat to take me! I'm so tiny that even on a small fishing boat, no one would even know I was there."

"Ah, but you won't be alone on this trip. There will be many other animals with you, and you will be noticed and needed on this trip," said the big turtle.

"It is time, Tuffy, that you take your place in our family and be given the knowledge that the Creator God has passed to me and to our family before me."

Tuffy heard the seriousness in his grandfather's voice, and he listened intently. "I am ready, Grandfather. I want to know all about the Creator God."

And so began Tuffy's full learning of all that his Grandfather knew. He then learned of the coming rain and how God planned to save only Noah and his family because God found them to be righteous."

"Grandfather, what does *righteous* mean?" he asked.

"It means that Noah has found favor with God because Noah loves and trusts in God, and worships only Him. It means that Noah is good and kind not only to his family but to others around him. He never speaks ill of anyone, and he helps those who need help."

"Is that what I am to do now?" asked Tuffy. "Am I to trust in God? But I already do, Grandfather! Ever since you and father told me about Him, I have loved and trusted the Creator God."

"Yes, I know that you have faith in our Creator," said Grandfather, "and that is why you have been given the gift of His Spirit that our family has had since the beginning. That is why you must now carry on with your task at hand and tell the animals of what is coming."

"I will do it, Grandfather!" said Tuffy, feeling very important now even with his tiny size. "But won't you be on the boat with us?" he asked.

"No," said the wise old turtle. "I am returning to the river. I came from the river, and I will go back to the river. It is you who must now carry on our work, our task of teaching the animals about our Creator. It is time for you to return to Noah and be ready."

"I'm going, Grandfather," Tuffy said. "But I will see you soon." And with that, he slowly made his way back to Noah.

When Tuffy Turtle returned to Noah's place on the river, he was surprised to see all the people gathered around Noah and his boat. They were all laughing and jeering at Noah and his sons for building such a monstrous boat in the middle of the desert.

"Where do you think you can put this thing?" they called out, laughing at the idea of this boat fitting in their river.

"You are a crazy old man," they yelled. "And you are making your sons crazy!" they added.

But Noah and his sons kept working, for the boat was nearly done.

Tuffy looked up at the sky and saw dark clouds gathering in the west, and he knew that what his grandfather had said was true. How he knew he didn't know, but he knew that the rains were coming and that he had to tell the animals.

As he waddled along the river-bank, he saw *her*, a beautiful little turtle he had noticed before. She was pale green with brown and gold speckles. She was coming toward him.

"Your grandfather sent me to find you," she said. "I'm Tanda, and he said you would take care of me in the days ahead."

Tuffy's heart fluttered, as he had never seen a turtle so beautiful. He gave thanks to his grandfather for sending her.

Then he gave thanks to the Creator God, for he knew that she was to be his partner on the boat and for the years to come.

Yes, he knew there would be many years ahead for them. He didn't know how or why, but he just knew that God would take care of them and see them through the coming rains and storm.

He knew that all would be well and that it was in God's hands, but it was up to him to carry God's words of promise to the animals. Words to drive away their fear of the coming storm. Words of comfort and strength that he must share.

Tuffy looked at Tanda and told her they had work to do. She nodded as if she already knew, and they headed back to Noah's home.

Chapter 2

Two by Two the Animals Came

As Tuffy and Tanda approached Noah's home, they saw a marvelous thing. Noah's sons were driving the animals, two by two, toward the finished boat. They heard Noah call out, "Come, bring them up to the Ark. Hurry! Time is running short."

So the animals were led, two by two, up into the Ark. Tuffy and Tanda hurried as fast as they could to be on the ark before the animals got there. Two lions entered, then two elephants, two ostriches, two donkeys, two goats, two penguins, two . . . well, you get the picture.

There were two of every living animal on the earth, two of every bird of the air, two of every fish in the sea, two of every bug and every creepy, crawling thing.

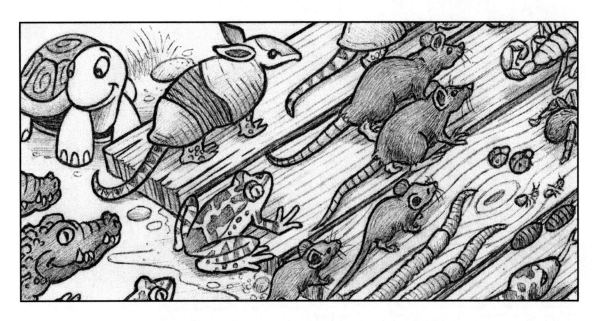

Two by two they entered the Ark, and Tuffy was there to greet each one and tell them not to be afraid or worry because the Creator God was with them. He would take care of them during the days ahead.

Now, most of the animals already knew of the coming rains. They knew that they were to go with Noah, because Grandfather Turtle had already prepared them, and they trusted Grandfather Turtle just as they had come to trust in the Creator God.

But there were a few who had some doubts about all they had heard. Rains that would not end. Going on a big boat. The world being forever changed.

The goats—a frisky male and female—had many questions, but they listened intently to Tuffy, and after the other animals told them that all was OK and that there was plenty of room for them, they entered the Ark.

The finicky pigs also entered rather hesitantly, but they entered.

There was only one who would not stop hopping around and claiming that there was no way he would get on a boat of any size for any reason.

Of course, Tuffy knew who that was right away: none other than J.R. Rabbit!

Tuffy had learned all about J.R. and the family of rabbits that had doubted and questioned the Creator of All from the very beginning. J.R. was part of the seventh generation of the Skeptirabbitus family of doubters.

"Hurry, J.R., we are waiting for you, and the rains are starting," said Tuffy as the first drops of rain splattered on the Ark's deck. "Everybody is on board, including Noah and all his family."

But J.R. wasn't about to be persuaded. He looked at Tuffy, then up at the big, BIG boat, and said, "Naw, naw. I think I'll stay on dry land."

"But J.R., the land isn't going to stay dry for very long," said Tuffy

"And just how do you know that?" asked J.R., for he was always full of questions.

Bible Stories according to Tuffy Turtle

"Because the Great Creator God has told Grandfather and me that we must go on the boat and be saved from the flood that is coming."

"Flood?" said J.R. "You said 'flood.' Get real, you crazy turtle. We live in

a desert. There's no flooding here." He looked up at the sky as more raindrops began to fall all around him. "A little rain never hurt anything. In fact, we need some rain. And anyway, turtle, just who is the 'Creator God' you talk about? Where did He come from?"

Tuffy was ready for such questions from J.R. Grandfather had told him all about J.R. and his family, and Tuffy knew he was ready for any question J.R. would ask.

"Well, I can't tell you where He came from," said Tuffy, "but I can tell you He is the God who created every-thing that ever was and ever will be."

"Oh yeah, well who made Him?" asked J.R.

Now, this question has been asked silently by many throughout the his-tory of the world by both man and animals, especially by the animals.

Two By Two The Animals Came

How does this God exist? But they had come to accept that the Creator God just *was*, always had been, and always would be. He just *was*!

Tuffy was ready for this question. "I can only tell you *who* God is, not who made Him."

"Yeah, and who is this God?" said J.R., wiggling his long ears.

"He is the one true Creator of everything that you see, feel, touch, and . . . and eat," said Tuffy, knowing that the thought of food would get J.R.'s attention.

"OK. You say He makes everything. If you make something, you can see it and touch it. So why can't I see and touch Him? Where is He?" J.R. asked as he looked about. "Is He on that . . . that boat?" J.R. said, pointing up at the boat and seeing the animals looking down at him.

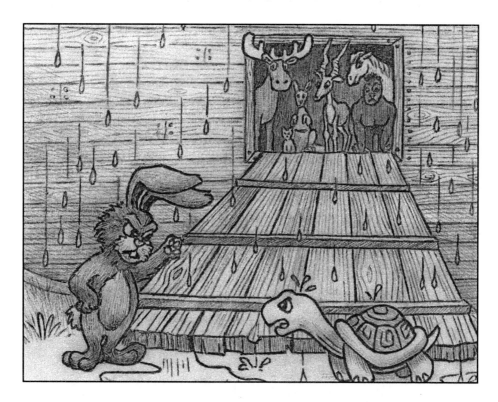

Bible Stories according to Tuffy Turtle

Some were on the deck and some were looking through the windows. All of them were shaking their heads at this silly little rabbit who wouldn't come out of the rain, for the rain was starting to fall fast and hard now.

"J.R., all I can tell you is that you must have faith in God. Trust that He will take care of you, and that He will provide for you on the Ark. Trust that He will take care of us during this storm and the many days ahead." Tuffy knew that there would be many, many dark, rainy days on the Ark.

"Faith, faith, faith!" said J.R. "That's all I've ever heard of about this God. 'You've gotta have faith.' Well, I only have faith in what I see," said J.R.

Just then, Tanda called from the door of the Ark.

"Tuffy, J.R., come on in out of the rain. I have some carrots and lettuce for you here. Don't let them get wet. And J.R., you have a friend waiting for you," she said as she looked at a tiny little rabbit sitting next to her.

J.R. took one look, then another. He couldn't quite decide if he wanted to look at the carrot or the little rabbit who was wiggling her ears at him.

Two By Two The Animals Came

Just then there was a loud crack of thunder, and a bold of lightning hit the ground behind J.R.

With a startled jump, he hopped right up into the Ark, with Tuffy waddling behind him.

After they entered, Noah closed the door of the Ark. The floodgates of heaven opened up, and the Ark drifted off down the river.

Chapter 3

Forty Days and Forty Nights

The rain seemed never to stop. The Ark seemed never to stop rolling and tossing in the waves. The thunder seemed to grow louder each night. And Noah's family seemed to be growing restless as they moved about their tasks, cleaning the stalls and feeding the animals.

The animals seemed relatively calm and quiet through it all. Oh, there was an occasional squeal, a little tweet, a soft braying, or a low, muted growl. But on the whole, they were talking among themselves and asking one basic question.

"When?" asked the big brown bear.

"How much longer?" the giraffe asked as she stretched her long neck through the window, getting herself and everyone near her wet.

"Will this rain never end?" whispered the pig, who wanted to roll in some wet mud.

"Forty days is *enough!*" wailed J.R. Rabbit. "Tell that God of yours I've *had it*!" he groaned at Tuffy.

Now Tuffy, while being young in years, was wise in the way of the Great Creator God. He had been taught by his grandfather and father, who were from the long line of Spiriturtleluses. They had been blessed by the Creator to understand His ways and to be able to share this with all the animals. They had been doing it for seven generations. Tuffy was of the seventh generation. And J.R. was of the seventh generation of his family known as the Skeptirabbituses.

This rare breed of rabbits were just not able to understand the ways of the Creator, nor were they able to have faith in God.

Tuffy knew that it didn't matter how many times they were told the story of the creation and God's care for it. It didn't matter how many times they were told of God's love for all of His creation. It didn't matter how many times they were told to have trust in the Creator and have faith. It just didn't matter to these family of skeptics. That is why they are called the Skeptirabbitus family.

So Tuffy knew it wouldn't matter now if he told J.R. what he knew. J.R. wouldn't believe it anyway. Tuffy knew that forty days was enough of the rain, and that after this night it would be over.

While Tuffy didn't know what would happen next, he knew that the rain would stop in the morning and that everything would be alright in the end. He had faith. He just wished he could share that with J.R. and somehow, some way, help J.R. to have this same faith. With a big sigh, he gave it a try.

"J.R., you must be patient like the rest of the animals. See how they don't moan and groan like you do. Even Noah and his family have faith in God. They know that all will be well, that the Creator is taking care of them . . . and you. Especially you," Tuffy said.

"Me? Me especially?" asked J.R. He like the sound of that. Was he something special to this strange God they all talked about? How could that be? He had never even seen or heard this God, so how could something not seen or known know him to be special?

"How is that, Tuffy? I mean, how am I special to this Creator God you always talk about?"

"J.R., all animals, all people, everyone, and everything is special to the Creator. You will see in the morning."

There! Tuffy had done it. He had let out that something would happen in the morning. The animals who were close to them and heard them talking perked up their ears and leaned forward to hear more.

"What's that, Tuffy? Something is going to happen in the morning?" asked the tiny mouse peeking out from some hay under the horses' hooves.

Tuffy looked around and smiled . . . well, as much as a little turtle can smile.

"You must all be patient, for you will see in the morning. That is all I know. That is what I believe, for I trust that God has something special planned for all of us in the morning. And now I am going to go to sleep so I can be ready when the sun comes out."

There! He had done it again. He'd let it slip that the sun was going to finally shine. He shook his head as he quickly waddled away—as quick as a turtle can.

He didn't know how he knew the sun was going to shine tomorrow. He just knew. He had faith that the Creator God would make it so.

Chapter 4

And the Sun Will
Come Out ... Today!

Forty days and forty nights had come and gone. There was an air of quiet excitement spreading through the animals. The Ark had stopped rocking. The wind had stopped howling. The thunder had stopped cracking. And the sound of rain had stopped beating on the Ark.

There was the sound of shuffling hoofs in the hay, of wings fluttering open, of claws scratching the floor, of tails switching, and of feathers being ruffled out. More birds started singing their songs, and suddenly there was a cacophony of noise as a burst of sunlight shot through a crack in an upper window.

Thump, thump, thump was heard throughout the Ark as J.R. came bounding down the aisle. "Tuffy! Tuffy! TUFFY!!" he called excitedly. "The sun! The sun came out!" he shouted for everyone to hear, as if they couldn't already see the sunlight filtering in throughout the Ark.

Noah and his sons were opening all the windows so they could see out, and a fresh breeze drifted through the warm, stale air of the Ark, which was soon replaced by the fresh smell of air after a good rain. What a rain it had been.

"Tuffy! Tuffy! *TUFFY!!* Where are you?" cried J.R.

All the animals looked around and asked each other, "Where is Tuffy?" But the little turtle was nowhere to be seen.

"Maybe he's fast asleep," said one.

"Did he fall overboard?" asked another.

"Perhaps he is hiding," said a third.

"He can't miss this!" said another.

"I'll find him!" said J.R. as he hopped up on the back of a friendly cow and began looking out an open window. "Oh! There you are, Tuffy," he said. "What are you doing out on the deck?" he asked as he jumped down through the window and sat beside the turtle.

"I'm thanking the Creator God for the sunshine," said Tuffy.

J.R. was quiet for a moment, which was unusual for J.R. "Thanking God," he said. He looked at the sun, a shining golden ball reflecting on the water. *Water*! Water was everywhere! All over! There was *no* land to be seen.

J.R. looked at Tuffy and said, "Well, now, your God's gone and done it, Tuffy. You can thank Him for the sun, alright. But He sure took away the land! Made it *ALL* disappear! Are you going to thank Him for that?" J.R. exclaimed, wiggling his ears. "What am I—what are *we all*—gonna do without land? I can't swim, you know. And I don't like to eat fish!" J.R. whined.

Tuffy looked at J.R. and could only say, "Be patient, J.R. The Creator God is in control, and He will take care of all of us. You'll see. Just be patient and have faith." And with that, Tuffy crawled away and back into the Ark.

"Faith! There he goes on with that *faith* word again," said J.R. "You can't eat faith!" He called after Tuffy.

But Tuffy was thinking to himself, *You may not eat faith, but faith will fill you on the inside, and you can live on and by and with faith.* If only J.R. could get it, could understand it. Tuffy slowly shook his head as he entered the Ark.

Meanwhile, Noah was already busy selecting a bird to fly out to see if there was land anywhere. The bird flew and flew and flew some more, but he always came back because he couldn't find anyplace to land. No tree, no rock, no little spot of land, nothing but water.

But then one day the dove came back with an olive branch. Noah and his family were very excited, for it meant that there was a tree growing somewhere.

All the animals picked up on the excitement, for they also knew that a tree had been found, and they understood what that meant. Land had been found.

All the birds were singing, hoofs were pounding, and squeals, snorts, and growls were heard throughout the Ark. No more quiet whispers and murmurings anymore.

Rejoicing was in the air as all the animals praised the Creator God and gave thanks.

Each day Noah sent the dove out, and one day it didn't come back. Noah knew that it was time to leave the Ark. He opened the door, dropped the long plank, and stepped out to a wondrously beautiful sight.

And The Sun Will Come Out ... Today!

Green grass, trees, and flowers of all colors were spread out before him as far as he could see. The hills, valleys, and mountains were all covered in the colors of the rainbow.

And there *was* a rainbow, a huge arch of color stretching from one side of the sky to the other. It was as if all the colors of the rainbow were falling down and mixing together to color the earth.

Noah fell to his knees and thanked God for such wonders.

"What is he doing?" asked Tanda to Tuffy.

"Is he crying?" asked the goat.

"Is he ill?" asked the leopard.

"Is he hurt? Did he fall down?" asked the panda bear.

"No," said Tuffy. "He is listening to his God, to the Creator God, and thanking Him for bringing us all safely through the storm. The Creator God is promising never to send a flood to the land again."

"How do you know this?" asked J.R.

"Do you see the rainbow in the sky?" said Tuffy, looking up at the sky.

"The Creator God put that rainbow in the sky as His promise to never destroy the earth again. He asked Noah to go out into the land with all of us and live in harmony and peace again."

"And," Tuffy added, quite seriously now, "the Creator God promised to be with us always."

"With us?!" said J.R. "Well, I'll thank this God for setting us free from that boat, but why couldn't He have done it forty days ago—even twenty days ago? I'll never know why He waited so long."

And with that, J.R. hopped down the board to the ground and hopped away, followed by a very plump rabbit and several little ones.

Yes, someday you will know, thought Tuffy. I don't know when or where or how, but someday you and yours will know the Creator God. Tuffy prayed to God, "Let it be so," as he followed all the other animals off the Ark and onto solid ground.

"Yes," said Tuffy, "I am standing on solid ground when I stand on faith in the Creator God." Then Tuffy and Tandy ambled away into the lush, green grass to find a new home.

Book 3: The Tower of Babel and the Tenth Generation of Tuffy

Chapter 1

Babel, Babel, Babel On

Oh, the noise. The dreadful noise. Tuffy tried to bury himself further into his shell to escape the noise, but it didn't work. At first it was the work, the constant work of the people trying to build a city, then a tower—that crazy ziggurat up to the heavens to reach God.

The pounding, pounding! The yelling back and forth, and back and forth! The constant rumbling and grumbling of the earth as the people dragged big stones upon big stones and built this monstrosity even higher into the heaven

Into the heavens, Tuffy laughed to himself. Didn't they know how hopeless their quest was, how impossible it was to build anything so high to reach the Creator God?

Didn't they know that they were now one people with one language and should be content with their lives in unity and peace? Their lives under the God of Creation.

But no! Tuffy sadly shook his head. He had heard from his father, his grandfather, and their fathers before them that these humans were strange indeed.

They were never satisfied with what they had, but were always trying to get more and more of anything and everything.

At least most of them. There had been some from the beginning of time that had trusted in and believed in the Creator God and His Goodness. There had been one that Tuffy had always heard about from his father's father's grandfather: Noah.

Now, *there* was a man of faith. Tuffy wished he knew a man who would gladly build and live on a boat with God as his provider rather than these silly men building a tower to reach the heavens to be closer to their God.

Tuffy was so lost in his thoughts that he didn't hear the loud commotion outside until he heard the unmistakable voice of J.R. Rabbit yelling into his shell.

"Tuffy! *Tuffy*! *Get out here*! Everyone's gone crazy! They're *all crazy*!"

Tuffy slowly peeked his head out; the noise was deafening. Unbelievably, incredibly, undeniably deafening, and a total mishmash of nonsensical, unimaginable sounds!

"Can you understand them?" J.R. yelled over the noise.

Tuffy slowly smiled. "Nope," he said. He didn't know who was sillier, J.R. for not understanding what was happening, or these people who tried to reach God—or *be* God—by building a magnificent tower to show off themselves or prove their greatness. *How silly these humans are,* he thought.

"What are you smiling at?" asked J.R., totally bewildered by what he was seeing and hearing all around them. "They're nuts!" he wailed.

"Yes, they are," replied Tuffy. "They still haven't learned to trust in God before and above all things," he said as he looked up at the tower, which seemed to be tottering and teetering side to side now . . . dangerously so!

"Come on, J.R., we'd better move out of the way. That tower is coming down!" Tuffy waddled off as quickly as he could.

J.R. was hopping right behind him, and he watched as the tower toppled to the ground, with people scattering and yelling everywhere.

"Tuffy, what in the world are they saying? I can't understand them anymore! What has them not trusting in this God you're always talking about have to do with it?"

Tuffy smiled to himself. *Everything,* he thought, but he knew that J.R. wouldn't get it. He never did seem to understand the concept or truth about the Creator of All that Is.

Tuffy knew that J.R. was from a long line of rabbits known as Skeptirabbituses because they questioned everything about the Creator. And Tuffy also knew that being a part of the Spiriturtlelus line of Faith Teachers, his job was to try to help J.R. along in his journey to trusting and believing in God. *Just maybe,* he thought, *this will be the story that works a miracle in J.R. to help him believe.*

He stopped and turned to J.R. "Come on, J.R., let me tell you a story about why there's all this confusion in people understanding each other. This just might help you understand the Power of God in your and their lives."

"Oh, great! There you go again, Tuffy, talking about this God of yours! What's so good about all this confusion and babbling going on, where no one can understand each other? I don't know who's crazier, you or them!" And saying that, J.R. hopped off into the noise.

Someday, J.R., you and yours will understand, Tuffy thought. *Someday, all in God's time and in God's ways. Someday . . .* And Tuffy turned to waddle off to his home and family.

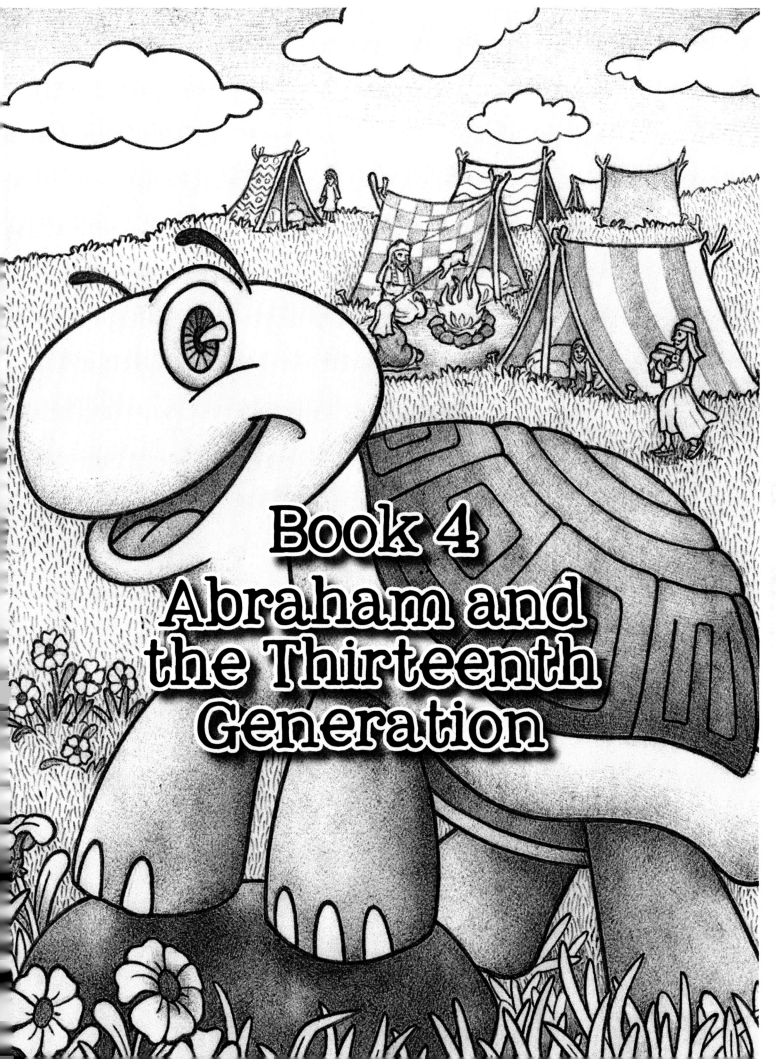

Book 4
Abraham and the Thirteenth Generation

Chapter 1

A Journey of Trust

Some people would say that the number thirteen is unlucky, but for one little turtle by the name of Tuffy, it was a very lucky number. And why is that? Well, I'll tell you.

You see, this little turtle is of the thirteenth generation of Tuffy Turtles that have been given a very special place by the Great Creator of All Things.

Ever since the first generation of Tuffy Turtles, this family had been called the Spiriturtlelus family because the Great Creator had blessed them with the ability to know and understand the love of God. It was the task of this family of turtles to share and tell all the animals about God. That is the name that the first Tuffy Turtle called the Great Creator, and that is the name that the animals had come to know as the Source of their being.

Now, how was it that this particular turtle felt that he was lucky? Well, he happened to live during the time of Abraham. Abraham was also a special person to the Creator God. God had Abraham and his whole family move from their homeland far in the north in a very fertile and lush land to an unknown land far, far, far away.

They traveled over mountains and into valleys, across rivers and through the desert for days and days, even months before they came to the land that the Creator God had promised to Abraham. Now, you may be asking how it was that a tiny, little turtle could make such a trip. Again, I shall tell you. It wasn't planned—or maybe it was by the Creator. But Tuffy was the pet of one of Abraham's nephew's daughters, who was named Aliaza, and she carried him with her all the way.

At night when Tuffy was let loose to roam and look for food, he would often be among the cattle and goats and donkeys that Abraham had brought along.

Now these big animals were tired, hungry, and thirsty at night, especially as they crossed the desert. They began to grumble and complain among themselves about this hard trip.

Tuffy would talk to the animals and tell them about the Creator God and His promise to Abraham to bring him to a special land of plenty. "But why?" they would ask in frustration and weariness. "Why would he want to leave his family and friends?"

Night after night, they asked, and Tuffy would patiently tell the story of how the Creator God had chosen Abraham, his family, and all their animals for a very special purpose.

"But why?" they would continually ask, for they had not yet come to understand this strange God of Abraham's—or Tuffy's, for that matter.

"You must be patient and trust," Tuffy explained over and over again. "Trust in the Creator God for He is in control and has only good in His plan for Abraham and for us too."

"How do you know such things?" they complained to Tuffy and to each other.

But it was a wise donkey who on one particular night said, "I may not understand it all, but I was in the field near Abraham when I heard him talking to someone alone in the dark."

"Who was it?" a skinny little goat whined.

"I don't know. I never saw anyone, but I heard Abraham asking the same question: 'Why must I move all my family and all my possessions and all my animals to a land I don't know?'"

"Ah, ah! So it's true then," said a very skeptical little rabbit who had accidentally been packed up with some household food items—or *was* it an accident?

The rabbit, called J.R., continued. "Abraham was talking to the air, to no one. It's true: he must be crazy!"

Now Tuffy was well familiar with J.R. Rabbit, as he also was of the thirteenth generation of the Skeptirabbitus family. Tuffy's father had explained to him about J.R.'s family's inability to grasp the meaning of the Creator God, even though for generation upon generation they had all tried to help the rabbits see the light of God's love and care for them.

"J.R., you know there is a reason for everything," Tuffy said. "We all know there is a reason for this trip, even though we may not understand it right now. We know that Abraham trusts his God, and we must also, for we trust Abraham. Isn't that right?" Tuffy asked all the animals.

There was some soft grumblings and mutterings, but finally they all nodded and said, "Yes, we trust Abraham."

The donkey said, "He is our caretaker and leader. Even though the trip has been long and difficult, he always has made sure we have water and food at night."

"That's right," said the goat, "We trust Abraham and we have come to trust his God also."

There was a long silence as J.R. hopped around them and looked at each in disbelief. "You have got to be kidding!" he cried. "You're all nuts like Abraham!"

This was too much for Tuffy. "J.R.!" he cried. "Why is it you have so little faith and trust in Abraham?" he asked. "You know and see him every day. You see how he cares for his family and for all of us. He even makes sure you get some cabbage from his own plate. How can you not trust that he cares for you?" Tuffy sounded very exasperated.

"Well," J.R. said, drooping his ears and lowering his head, embarrassed, "I never thought of Abraham caring for me." He perked up. "But how do I know this God of his cares for me? I don't see Him around here."

At this, all the animals groaned and shook their heads, for they had now come to know and understand this God who couldn't be seen or heard. They trusted in this God because Abraham trusted in this God.

"Rabbit!" they said in unison. "Go away with you doubts and questions, and leave us in peace," they cried.

At all the noise, Abraham suddenly appeared among them. "Hush, my babies," he said.

He always called the animals his "babies" even though there were very few babies among them.

"It is all right," he said, calming them. "Tomorrow we will be in the land promised to me and to my family. This long, hard trip will be over, and you will all have more grass and water then you can imagine. We will rest and be happy."

Abraham looked around and saw J.R. "Ah, little rabbit, you are out here in the dark. Come with me and have the carrot I saved for you."

A Journey Of Trust

After saying that, he scooped up J.R. and walked away. J.R. looked back at the animals and wiggled his ears in delight.

Tuffy watched and said to the animals, "See, if Abraham can care for that silly rabbit, then God can surely care for us." He looked around at all the animals, as if asking them to disagree, and they all nodded in agreement. Then he slowly crawled back to Aliaza's tent, for tomorrow would be a great day!

Book 5
Deborah and the Twentieth Generation

Chapter 1

Deborah as the Judge

It was noisy. It was too noisy. It was so noisy that Tuffy tucked himself further into his shell, which was pretty hard to do. Noise and commotion were hard for Tuffy to handle these days. He was growing old, and he could feel it in his bones—well, if he had any bones, that is. He was large, and pulling himself all the way into his shell was hard enough. If only Deborah had just kept quiet!

Deborah was the people's judge. Tuffy had sat near this tree for many years now, as had Deborah. She came to the spot nearly every day to listen to the people complain or ask questions.

He listened to her wisdom, as did many people. He came to trust the words of Deborah as she helped and guided people in solving their problems, disagreements, and struggles. These people had many disagreements!

Through the years, Tuffy had come to understand why the people came to her for help. He began to understand and know that the Creator God was with her and spoke through her. He didn't know how he knew, he just knew.

The Creator God had been quiet for many years, and Tuffy wondered if the God of Moses and Joshua was angry with His people. Ever since Joshua had led the people in victory at Jericho and brought the people into the Promised Land, things had gone astray. Life had gone wrong.

The people had turned from their God, who had freed them from slavery in Egypt. These people had stopped worshipping the Creator God, who had brought them safely out of the desert after forty years of wandering under the guidance of their great leader, Moses.

Moses, Tuffy thought to himself. He had heard so many stories about Moses from his father and grandfather, stories passed down from generation to generation of his family of Spiriturtlelus turtles. The turtles who had walked or been carried by the people of the Creator God. People He had chosen as His own special people, just as his family of turtles had been chosen to share the story of the Creator and of His love and care for all of His creation.

Tuffy had heard of his great, great, great, great, great . . . oh, he couldn't remember how far back it went, but he had heard the stories of the Great Flood and how Noah and his family had been saved along with two of every animal and bird, fish, and creepy, crawling thing. *Why them?* Tuffy thought. He remembered that they had been a nuisance every time they tried to crawl into his shell.

Tuffy opened his eyes with a start. The noise was louder. Closer. Sharper. Urgent. FRANTIC!

He focused his eyes, which was getting harder to do these days due to his age.

He saw two eyes, two very large eyes, two very, VERY large eyes staring back at him.

Oh, it's J.R., thought Tuffy. He had heard stories about the J.R. in the Garden of Abundance and Beauty when the Creator God made everything. He heard how J.R. just couldn't understand faith. He also had heard about the J.R. on the Ark during the Great Flood and about how impatient that J.R. had been.

He also had heard about J.R.'s great, great, great, great, great . . . whatever! Tuffy had heard that that J.R. had done nothing but complain during the forty years of wandering in the desert.

Tuffy had a tendency to get lost in his thoughts these days, but this J.R. was relentlessly pounding on his shell. "What is it, J.R.?" Tuffy asked as he slowly and reluctantly pulled himself out of his shell. He tried to hide his annoyance, almost dreading to find out what was upsetting J.R.

"What is it?" J.R. groaned in disbelief. "Do you see all these people? I almost got trampled trying to get to you!" he cried.

"Yes, yes." Tuffy nodded. "I see them," he said as he squinted off into the distance, seeing a multitude of people gathered around Deborah. She was sitting where she always sat, under the tree. She was quiet as the rest of them all seemed to talk at once.

"They're talking war!" wailed J.R.

Noise. More noise, thought Tuffy.

"Yes, I know," said Tuffy. "Judah ben Bird told me. See, she's sitting above Deborah in the tree. And Mannaniah Mouse is hiding under the rock next to her. She hid in some basket and came in with the tribe of Mannessah. Levan the Lion also comes at night to tell me what is happening with the tribe of the Levites. And that silly Simon the Goat interrupts my sleep all the time, telling me what the tribe of Simeon is up to." Tuffy let out a big sigh.

"Oh yeah, I know that goat," said J.R. "All he does is say 'Baa, baa, baa,' to everything. I was down at their camp the other night and heard the men of Simeon talking with the men of Dan. Yikes! Do they like to fight!"

"Yes, so I heard. The tribe of Dan nearly killed off the tribe of Benjamin." Tuffy shook his head. These were the people of the Creator God, and all they had done since coming to the Promised Land was fight among themselves and fight with their neighbors.

Tuffy gave a big sigh. *Will it never end?* he wondered.

Deborah As The Judge

Again he was jolted out of his thoughts by J.R.

"So what's gonna happen? Are they all going to war again? I'll have to hide with all my family, and where are we gonna hide?" J.R. was impatiently thumping his foot now. "And what are you gonna do with all your family?" he asked.

"They are safe in a cave not far from here," answered Tuffy. He knew he had to keep all his little—and not so little—turtles safe. Someday one of them would carry on the Spiriturtlelus tradition of telling the story of the Creator God.

The noisy people sounded impatient and angry. Deborah's voice was calm and steady. But Tuffy could see that some of the people were already leaving, some in anger, some in confusion, some in sadness.

"What's going on now, Tuffy?" J.R. was looking over his shoulder at the commotion of people picking up their things and leaving in groups.

"Well," said Tuffy, "Deborah and her general, Barak, have been trying to unite all the different tribes to fight the Canaanites, who have been raiding into their tribal land of Issachar."

"Wowzer!" J.R. whispered. "Looks like there's gonna be a big, BIG war now." Looking at Tuffy, he continued. "Are they all going to get ready to fight?"

"No," answered Tuffy, shaking his head. "No, the other tribal leaders want nothing to do with Deborah and Barak's war."

J.R. looked skeptically at Tuffy. "And just how do you know that?" he asked sarcastically. "You can't—you couldn't have heard them talking." He wiggled his ears as if challenging Tuffy to answer him.

"Judah ben Bird told me early this morning. She heard Deborah and Barak talking with a few of the other leaders, and they all said they didn't want to get involved."

Involved, thought Tuffy to himself. *If only these people would listen to their God, the Creator God, and know how involved He was in their lives. If only they would trust that Deborah listens to the voice of God, would they then get involved?*

J.R. brought Tuffy back to the present with a loud *humph.* "Well, if they're not going to get involved, and they're all going back to their own homelands, I'm gonna go see that my family is alright and maybe go take some of the little ones out to look for some fresh greens, like wild lettuce."

And without waiting for Tuffy's response, J.R. hopped away.

That's not a bad idea, thought Tuffy as he slowly waddled away. He hadn't been home to the cave in some time, and he wondered how Tabitha and all the little turtles were doing without him.

Well, of course, he knew they were doing just fine. He didn't know how he knew, he just knew that the Creator God would take care of them and of all of His creation and His people, just   as He always did.

Chapter 2

Deborah as the War Leader

uffy sat basking in the warm April sunshine. He had spent the last several months in the back of a cave, huddled for warmth with his family.

Snow had come to the high hill country of Issachar, and they were lucky to share the cave with a slumbering bear.

Word had come via the Izzy Lizard network of lizards, geckos, and salamanders who had raced among the rocks that Deborah had marched off to war, leading General Barak's army.

That's strange, thought Tuffy, *that a woman, especially a gentle woman like Deborah, should be leading an army.* But one of the cave salamanders had told him that the army would not march against the Canaanite army of Sisera unless Deborah led them. Tuffy knew that Deborah would not do it unless it was the Great Creator's will.

And so Tuffy talked with his family and said his farewells. He promised to come back home soon. Well, "soon" was not a word that fit Tuffy these days—or years, for that matter. He was old and gray.

Well, turtles can't be gray, but he had seen people grow old and gray, so he figured he must be old and gray too. His eyesight was fading, so maybe his molten-green shell was turning gray.

Tuffy slowly crawled out of the cave and worked his way down the hillside to the tree where Deborah always sat and met with her people. It wasn't far, but for an old turtle, it was far enough. After a few days, which seemed like forever, he arrived at the tree and lay soaking up the sunshine, lost in the comfort of the warmth.

Suddenly he heard *that* sound again. "Wake up! WAKE UP you slumbering slug!"

Tuffy opened one eye and saw the shape of an old gray rabbit in front of him.

"Oh, J.R., must you always pounce on me?" he almost whined at J.R. But turtles do not whine, especially wise, old turtles, and Tuffy was both wise and old.

"Is this the way to greet me after all these months? By pouncing on me?" asked Tuffy. "What's got your hairs ruffled?" Tuffy chuckled inwardly at his little joke.

"It's happened! It's happened again! The army lost. Oh, grief!" wailed J.R. "We're all lost now. They're gonna come and get us! *US*! *Me*! I'll probably end up as someone's stew, and that is *not* in my plans! And what of all my little rabbits. They're too young to be someone's tasty meal!" "Relax, relax, J.R., that's not going to happen."

"How can you say that? The army lost and they ran away. I heard it from that silly goat."

"I tell you, it's going to be alright," Tuffy said with confidence. "I have it from a most reliable source." Tuffy nodded with more confidence, and he began to wonder where this was coming from. But then again, he knew. He didn't know how he knew, but he knew. "I can assure you that everything will be alright. Barak's army will win."

"WIN!" J.R. was near panic state now. "Win?! That ragtag, hit-and-run bunch of . . . bunch of . . ." J.R. was left wordless, which was very strange for him. "All they do is strike and run, strike and run. They're good at running!" he said disdainfully.

"Well, they won't run this time. In fact, they didn't run away. There was a big battle, and they won. God promised them they would win, and to ensure it, Deborah was to march in front of the army." Tuffy was a bit breathless from talking for so long.

"Are you crazy?" J.R. fairly howled—if a rabbit could howl. "That same Deborah who sits under that tree?"

J.R. pointed to the tree as he hopped around in disbelief. "A woman leading an army?!" J.R. dropped his head, shaking it back and forth. "Oh, this is getting worse and worse!"

Tuffy looked at J.R. and wondered when this rabbit, so full of skepticism, would come to trust in the Creator God. "J.R., you have to have faith, even a little faith," he said gently. "You have to trust in God that He will take care of His people—and us in the process."

But J.R. would have nothing of this 'trust in God' talk. "Trust God? What God?! Where is He?" J.R. said, looking around. "I don't see Him around here!"

Tuffy heaved a big sigh. "Well, maybe if you had sat and listened to Deborah pray, you would realize that there is nothing to fear. God is in control."

J.R. stopped hopping around and looked at Tuffy in disbelief. "Are you for real?" he asked. "There you go talking about this God again. From what you say, there is only one god. Solo, alone. But the Canaanites have many gods. So who is more powerful? One or many?" And J.R. cocked his head as if challenging Tuffy to get out of this question.

But Tuffy was ready. He and J.R. always seemed to have the same discussion. Tuffy believed in the Creator God, and J.R. didn't. Tuffy came from a long line of believers, the Spiriturtlelus family. And J.R. came from a long line of doubters, skeptics called the Skeptirabbitus family.

Someday J.R. would come to learn the truth, but Tuffy wasn't sure it was going to be that day. "Well, J.R., you will see that the God of Deborah's people is in control. You will see that this God will take care of His people and you, and will give you a good life too."

J.R. looked at Tuffy rather skeptically. "Do you have a good life?" he asked. "Do you think living in that shell is a good life?" J.R.'s tone was a bit softer now. He didn't really want to hurt his old friend's feelings.

"Of course I do," Tuffy answered cheerily. "I have everything I need, and I thank the Creator God every day for caring for me—for all of us. Even you, J.R. And you will see; the army will come home victorious. And that's that." With saying that, Tuffy slowly pulled himself back into his shell.

J.R. looked into the shell, then looked around, looked around again, looked up and down, then called back into Tuffy's shell, saying, "Well, maybe

I'll go sit under that tree where Deborah always sat. Maybe this God of hers and of yours"—and he peeked into the shell, speaking loudly—"maybe this God will speak to me." And he hopped away.

Well, maybe He will, thought Tuffy. Stranger things have happened.

And he closed his eyes in sleep.

Book 6
David and
the Twenty-Third
Generation of Tuffy

Chapter 1

The Twenty-Third Psalm

This is the story of the twenty-third generation of Tuffy Turtles, who were given the gift of knowledge and wisdom of the Creator God. The twenty-third generation of the family, known as the Spiriturtleluses, had been given the calling of sharing God's love and acceptance with all the animals.

This is how the twenty-third Tuffy came to know and follow the great King David of Israel.

You see, he just happened to be in the field where David was watching his father's sheep when Samuel came to anoint him as the new king of Israel. Tuffy was quite amazed, as he already knew that there was another king named Saul who had turned from God and angered Him.

So Tuffy was intrigued, and from that day on he followed David as best he could, which wasn't easy being a little turtle. He wasn't able to follow all of David's battles against the Philistines, but he was there when David brought down the giant Goliath with a stone.

He wasn't there when David fought with the Philistines against the old king, Saul. But he heard from the animal runners the story of David's great victory and how he had finally become king.

Tuffy was fortunate to live in the garden of King David's palace in Jerusalem. He was able to hear and see David as he struggled to understand God's plan for him and his people. He heard David's songs of lament and praise.

This story is about one of the most loved *Psalms* as they were called, and how Tuffy tried to share it with another one of his long-time friends, J.R. Rabbit.

You see, J.R. was from the twenty-third generation of rabbits known as the Skeptirabbitus family. They were called this because they just didn't seem to get it regarding having faith in God and understanding His love for all His Creation.

But let's stop and listen to what happened when Tuffy tried to share the twenty-third Psalm with his friend, J.R. Rabbit.

Tuffy began, "The Lord is my shepherd, I shall not want."

"Want! All I want is a carrot right now," said J.R. impatiently.

"Oh, J.R., there is more to life than carrots, you know," said Tuffy.

The Twenty-third Psalm

"Like what?" asked J.R.

"Well, God leads you to green pastures, to green gardens, if you like."

"I like," said J.R. "Yes, I like very much."

"And he leads you to fresh running streams."

"Yeah, that's OK too," said J.R., quite enjoying what he was hearing now.

"He leads you on the right path, for His name's sake," continued Tuffy.

"Right path . . . yup! Always to the best cabbage patch!"

"J.R., will you listen to King David's Psalm?" asked Tuffy.

"A what?" asked J.R.

"A Psalm. It's a song he sings in this very garden when he is feeling good, when he is feeling sad, when he is happy, or when he is feeling troubled. It comforts him," explained Tuffy. "Now may I continue?"

"OK, OK, go on. I'm all ears!" said J.R. as he wiggled his long ears.

Bible Stories according to Tuffy Turtle

And so, Tuffy continued. "Even though I walk through the darkest valley, I fear no evil, for You are with me; Your rod and Your staff comfort me."

"I have no idea what that means," said J.R.

Now, Tuffy, being of the twenty-third generation of turtles dealing with the long line of skeptical rabbits, just sighed and said a silent prayer that someday, somehow, the Creator God would help this rabbit understand. And not only understand, but come to have faith in the Creator God and His Goodness.

"J.R., if you would just open your heart to our Creator God, you would understand how King David finds comfort in his faith in God, and perhaps you'd find comfort in that faith too."

"There you go again," said J.R., "talking about that 'faith' thing."

"Alright, J.R., just listen to what King David said in his song," said Tuffy. "You prepare a table before me . . ."

"Hey! I like that," interrupted J.R. "A table full of carrots and lettuce, and maybe even some celery. Yes! I'd like that. Where is this table?" said J.R., looking about excitedly.

The Twenty-third Psalm

"J.R. You're not listening with you head and heart," said Tuffy. "This is about God providing what you need."

"I need a table full of—" He was abruptly cut off by the turtle.

"Yes, I know. You only think of your stomach. But this is about God taking care of you, of David, of all of us. That's what this is about. Now will you listen?" asked Tuffy, slowly shaking his head in frustration.

"OK, OK, OK," said J.R. "This God prepares a table for . . . I mean, before me. Then what?"

"And my cup runneth over—" said Tuffy before being cut off by J.R.

"You lost me on that one, Tuffy. I don't have a cup. I don't even know what a cup is!" replied a very perplexed J.R.

"What it means, J.R., is that God is good to you. He supplies you with all that you need, each and every day," explained Tuffy.

"Oh, God does that, does He?" said J.R. "How come I never see this God? I sure would like to, you know. I sure would like to tell Him what I really would like to have. Maybe not every day, but some days."

Tuffy, slowly shaking his head at J.R.'s not being able to understand God's love, continued. "Surely goodness and mercy shall follow me all the days of my life, and I shall dwell in the house of the Lord forever."

Tuffy ended this great and beloved Psalm of David and looked at J.R.

J.R., well, he just sat and looked at Tuffy, slowly shaking his head and wondering what in the world this strange Turtle was talking about. *Goodness . . . Good* meant lots of carrots and all the things he liked to eat. *Mercy . . .* Well, J.R. had no idea what that meant.

And to "dwell in the house of the Lord." Well, if he couldn't see this God of Tuffy's, then he obviously couldn't see this "house" either.

With that thought, J.R. just turned around and hopped off, looking for some carrots, of course.

Tuffy watched J.R. and said another silent prayer that the Creator God would show love and mercy to this funny but crazy little rabbit, then he went back into his shell to think on all of God's goodness.

Book 7
The Prophets and the Seventh Generation of Tuffy Turtle

Isaiah 41 and Micah 6:8

Chapter 1

I Say It, You Do It!

uffy looked out from his shell. It was a warm, sunny day in Jerusalem. The sunshine was much needed after a cold March. J.R. Rabbit, his companion for many, many years, slumbered beside him.

Too long to remember, thought Tuffy. They had seen much, shared much, and suffered much in the past years. Wars with Syria had come and gone, and now the great nation of Assyria was threatening the people of Judah.

The people of the Creator God had turned from their worship of and devotion to Him, the God of their ancestors, and they had suffered for it.

But just like the rabbit sleeping beside him, they just didn't get it.

They didn't understand that they had not only disappointed the Creator but angered Him also.

Bible Stories according to Tuffy Turtle

Tuffy had been around for so long that he knew of an earlier prophet, Isaiah, who had spent years warning the people of Judah to turn and repent from their ways. Isaiah had called them to return to worship the one true God. But this Isaiah had also hoped for, and believed in, the Messiah, the Savior, who would one day come and rescue the people.

Rescue, thought Tuffy. *Are they really worth it?* He had seen too much of the meanness of the people over the years. He had lost some of his own family to them, just as J.R. had. When famine hit, these people had gone after the turtles for food. Tuffy had barely escaped several times, and he had learned to hide his children after that.

J.R. had not been so lucky at first. But he eventually learned to hide  his family, as these strange people seemed to like rabbit stew no matter what.

There were times over the many years that J.R. and Tuffy had lost touch, but they always seemed to find each other. And now, as they rested in the warm sunshine, Tuffy, moved to the opening of his shell and looked over at his old friend.

"Psst, J.R., wake up," he said softly. "J.R., have you heard the news?" he asked.

J.R. sat up with a start. "What news?" he asked, startled. "Is there another war happening?" He looked about anxiously.

"No, no," said Tuffy, shaking his head. "I hear that there is another prophet in the land."

I Say It, You Do It!

"Yeah, yeah," said J.R. "I told you about him. He's called Micah, and he's telling these people to turn from their ways and come back to God, just like Isaiah did.

You know," J.R. continued, rather disappointed, for he liked action over talk, "all those so-called 'prophets' do is talk. Why don't they raise an army to fight the Assyrians?" If J.R. could have wailed, he would have, but he was too old. But his voice was so feeble, he sounded like he was wailing anyway.

"J.R., will you never learn?" asked Tuffy. "Don't you remember the message from God that Isaiah told to these people? 'You are my servant, I have chosen you and not cast you off; do not fear, for I am with you; do not be afraid, for I am your God. I will strengthen you; I will uphold you with my victorious right hand.'"

"Well," J.R. huffed, "this God of theirs—of yours—must have forgotten that He said that! Look where it's gotten them. If this God of theirs chose them"—J.R. lowered his head, shaking it—"for what? For this?" And he looked over the barren land, still shaking his head.

Sadly, Tuffy said, "He's your God, too, J.R. You mustn't forget that."

"You're all crazy! Tuffy, come and live in the real world!" J.R. cried. "This God doesn't care about these people. Who would? They don't care about each other, so why does this God of yours care about them?"

But Tuffy knew from over the years that J.R. really did take after his ancestors, the Skeptirabbitus line of doubting rabbits. From the beginning of time, this had been true. Tuffy had learned from his father and grandfather that these rabbits just didn't understand faith.

Bible Stories according to Tuffy Turtle

It was up to his family of turtles, the Spiriturtlelus family, to help all the animals learn about the Creator God. They were to tell about the goodness and love of the Creator for all of His creation. They were to teach how to have faith and trust in the Creator, and that meant for this rabbit too!

But somewhere in those first years in the Garden of Abundance and Beauty, this rabbit family had never caught on to having faith.

"It's magic," had been the cry of these rabbits throughout history, and they just didn't believe in faith. And now, seventy generations later, they still didn't get it.

"J.R.," Tuffy continued, "you yourself heard the words of the prophet Micah, and you told me . . . remember?" Tuffy hoped that J.R.'s memory would recall those words.

J.R. slowly lifted his head and looked at Tuffy rather sheepishly. "Yeah, something to do about three things that this God wants from His people."

"Do you remember what those are?" asked Tuffy.

"Yeah, yeah, yeah," said J.R., nodding his head. "'Seek justice, do kindness, and walk humbly with God.'" J.R. looked at Tuffy. "How could I forget that, Tuffy, when you keep reminding me?!"

"Well, if I have to remind you, just think how often God has to remind His people. They are a thick-headed and stubborn people. But they will learn someday, just as I hope you learn, J.R."

"Well, don't get your hopes too high on that one, Tuffy. These people are never gonna learn." And with that, J.R. hopped away.

I Say It, You Do It!

Tuffy watched J.R. hop away and thought to himself, *Well, in God's time they will, J.R., just as in God's time, you will.*

And Tuffy slowly turned and waddled off to his favorite rock. He didn't know why it was his favorite, but he felt close to the Creator God when he was there. *Please Creator, he silently prayed, Come soon to this land of trouble and bring peace and harmony to people's lives. Open their minds to know Your Presence and open their hearts to know and receive Your Love.*

Little did Tuffy know that it would be nearly 400 years before the Creator God would enter the lives of His people again as a tiny baby born in Bethlehem just as the prophets had said. But that's another story in the Tuffy Turtle's family history.

Author's Page

Hi everybody!! J.R. Rabbit here!

I want to introduce the brain behind my creation. But first, I am the original J.R. Rabbit and you'll find the history of my family of 'Skeptirabbitus" in this book. I've been one of the 'headliners' running around in the mind of Joni Lundin McNamara for about 20-plus years. I share this space with a bunch of other characters who have been around for a l-o-o-o-n-g time before I came on 'stage'. My chief job in Joni's life is to create mayhem! You see, J.R. is for Jack Rascal, not Jack Rabbit!

Joni has been a professional puppeteer for nearly 35 years as owner/director of GEM PUPPET PRODUCTIONS/ARK ANGEL PUPPETS. She gets an idea and the rest of us characters are off with creating stories. We have performed in schools, churches, and for businesses with all original plays written by Joni. You name it, we've done it. But I'm supposed to talk about Joni and all the stories I've, I mean, we've done.

So, Joni is a graduate of Valparaiso University with a degree in Theology. She has lived in Africa and Europe and has traveled literally around the world more times than I can count. (Remember, I'm a rabbit and can't count anyway!) Her husband, Robert, is a retired pastor who now serves as a hospital chaplain in WY where they live. They have two grown children who were raised in a house full of puppets, not pets! Well, there were pets, but no rabbits, so they don't count!

Joni has retired from actively performing with her puppets but one never knows when one of us characters might pop out in public again! With five grandchildren, w-e-l-l, us characters are itching to get active! You see, even in retirement, she can't get away from us!

We are very active in turning her puppet plays, written to "tickle the hearts of all ages," into stories to be read and shared. The stories from the Bible are from the viewpoint of my family of skeptics ("Skeptirabbitus" as we love to question everything) along with my life-long friend, Tuffy Turtle who claims to have a special relationship with God and the Holy Spirit (the "Spiriturtlelus" family).

We travel through history from Creation to . . . well, God's Love and involvement with His Creation never ends, so stay tuned for more!

You can reach me, I mean, Joni, at jonimcnamara.com.

CPSIA information can be obtained
at www.ICGtesting.com
Printed in the USA
FFOW05n0121041117

9 781545 616659